# THE
# UNSTOPPABLE
# ENTREPRENEUR
## Unlocking Your Full
## Potential for Success

**Maxwell E. Uduafemhe, PhD.**

# DEDICATION

To my loving family,

Thank you for your unwavering support and encouragement throughout my writing journey. Your belief in me and my dreams has been a constant source of motivation. This book would not have been possible without your love and guidance.

# CONTENTS

# ACKNOWLEDGMENTS

With deep humility and gratitude, I dedicate "THE UNSTOPPABLE ENTREPRENEUR: Unlocking Your Full Potential for Success" to God. His grace and guidance have allowed me to understand and navigate the world of entrepreneurship successfully.

I am grateful for the knowledge, skills, and strength that He has bestowed upon me, which have helped me overcome obstacles and continue on this journey. I acknowledge that without His unwavering support, I would not have achieved the success that I enjoy today.

I pray that this book will inspire and guide others to realize their full potential, just as God has enabled me to do so. I remain eternally grateful for His blessings and guidance, which have been the guiding light in my entrepreneurial journey.

# Chapter 1

# Introduction

You have embarked on an exciting journey filled with challenges, risks, and opportunities as an entrepreneur. Entrepreneurship is not for the faint of heart, but the rewards can be enormous for those willing to take the risk and realize their full potential. In this chapter, we will look at the entrepreneurial journey, the mindset of a successful entrepreneur, and the importance of realizing your full potential for success.

## The Journey of Entrepreneurship

Entrepreneurship is more than just starting a business; it is a multifaceted journey that necessitates meticulous planning, unwavering determination, and unwavering resilience. It is about identifying a problem, developing a solution, and developing a sustainable business model that can thrive in today's competitive business landscape.

The entrepreneurial journey begins with an idea or a vision. It is the epiphany that occurs when you recognize an opportunity or a market gap. However, it takes much more than an idea to bring it to fruition. It entails conducting market research, creating a comprehensive business plan, securing funding, assembling a team, and navigating the legal, financial, and operational complexities of running a business.

As an entrepreneur, you will face numerous difficulties along the way. These may include intense competition, cash flow management, marketing and sales, hiring and retaining talent, scaling the business, and overcoming unexpected obstacles. The entrepreneurial journey can be filled with ups and downs, but it is the ability to overcome these challenges and persevere in the face of adversity that distinguishes successful entrepreneurs from the rest.

## Understanding the Mindset of an Entrepreneur

Every successful entrepreneur has a distinct mindset that distinguishes them from others. This mindset is defined by a set of characteristics, attitudes, and behaviors that fuel their drive, creativity, and resilience. Understanding and cultivating this entrepreneurial mindset is critical to realizing your full potential.

A strong sense of purpose is an important component of the entrepreneurial mindset. A clear vision and a sense of mission guide the decisions and actions of successful entrepreneurs. They are deeply committed to making a positive impact on the world through their idea or business. This sense of purpose gives them the motivation and resilience they need to overcome obstacles and stay focused on their goals.

A willingness to take risks is another important aspect of the entrepreneurial mindset. Entrepreneurs recognize that taking calculated risks is an essential component of the entrepreneurial journey. They are not afraid to push themselves outside of their comfort zones and embrace uncertainty because they understand that risks can lead to opportunities and growth. Successful entrepreneurs, on the other hand, do not take risks lightly; they carefully evaluate and manage risks, balancing them with potential rewards.

The entrepreneurial mindset must also include elements of innovation and creativity. Entrepreneurs are constantly looking for new and unique ways to disrupt the status quo, challenge conventions, and create value. They are not afraid to think outside the box, to devise novel solutions, and to embrace change. To stay ahead of the curve, they are constantly learning, adapting, and iterating their ideas and businesses.

Another important characteristic of successful entrepreneurs is a strong work ethic. Entrepreneurship necessitates perseverance, dedication, and hard work. Entrepreneurs are willing to invest the time, effort, and energy required to establish and expand their businesses. They are motivated by a strong desire to succeed and are willing to go above and beyond to achieve their objectives. They recognize that success does not happen overnight, and they are willing to put in the necessary effort and make the necessary sacrifices to make their vision a reality.

Furthermore, entrepreneurs have a mindset of continuous learning. They are constantly hungry for knowledge and looking for ways to improve themselves and their businesses. They are enthusiastic learners who welcome feedback, are willing to learn from mistakes, and are dedicated to personal and professional development. They recognize that the business landscape is constantly changing, and that staying relevant necessitates ongoing learning and adaptation.

Finally, successful entrepreneurs are resilient. They recognize that failures and setbacks are unavoidable on the entrepreneurial path. They do not, however, let failure define or deter them from achieving their goals. Failures are viewed as valuable learning opportunities, and they respond with renewed determination and resilience. They have a positive mindset that allows them to persevere in the face of obstacles, setbacks, and uncertainties in order to achieve their vision.

## The Importance of Unlocking Your Full Potential for Success

Unlocking your full potential as an entrepreneur is critical to your entrepreneurial success. When you maximize your strengths, overcome limitations, and unleash your creativity, innovation, and drive, you are able to maximize your potential. You are able to perform at your peak, capitalize on opportunities, and overcome challenges with resilience and determination.

Unlocking your full potential also allows you to discover new possibilities and push the limits of what you previously thought was possible. It improves your ability to think critically, solve problems, and make sound decisions. It gives you the ability to take calculated risks, embrace change, and adapt to changing business dynamics. When you realize your full potential, you are no longer constrained by self-doubt, fear, or external obstacles, but instead have the confidence and capability to pursue your dreams and achieve your goals.

Furthermore, realizing your full potential as an entrepreneur allows you to make a positive difference in your company, team, and the world around you. It enables you to lead authentically, inspire and motivate others, and foster an environment of innovation and growth. It gives you the ability to form meaningful relationships, leverage your networks, and create opportunities for yourself and others. When you reach your full potential, you become a positive change agent and contribute to the greater good.

To summarize, realizing your full potential entails not only achieving personal success, but also making a positive impact on your business, team, and the world. It is about becoming your best self and leveraging your unique strengths, mindset, and capabilities to achieve your entrepreneurial goals and make a meaningful difference. In the following chapters, we will look at practical strategies, tools, and insights to help you realize your full entrepreneurial potential and achieve unstoppable success.

## Chapter 1 Takeaways

1. Entrepreneurship is a multifaceted journey that necessitates meticulous planning, perseverance, and resilience.

2. A successful entrepreneur's mindset includes a sense of purpose, a willingness to take risks, innovation and creativity, a strong work ethic, a mindset of continuous learning, and resilience.

3. Unlocking your full potential as an entrepreneur is critical to your entrepreneurial success.

4. Realizing your full potential allows you to maximize your strengths, overcome limitations, unleash your creativity and drive, and make a positive difference in your business, team, and the world.

5. In the following chapters, we will look at practical strategies, tools, and insights to help you realize your full entrepreneurial potential and achieve unstoppable success.

# Chapter 2

# Discovering Your Passion

Passion is a strong motivator that fuels the entrepreneurial journey. When you are enthusiastic about what you do, you are more likely to be dedicated, motivated, and persistent in achieving your objectives. Discovering and utilizing your passion is a critical step in realizing your full entrepreneurial potential. In this chapter, we'll look at strategies for discovering your passion, reflecting on your interests and strengths, identifying your purpose and mission, and turning your passion into a viable business idea.

## Reflecting on Your Interests and Strengths

Reflecting on your interests and strengths is one of the first steps in discovering your passion as an entrepreneur. What do you genuinely care about? What activities or topics do you naturally gravitate toward and enjoy spending time on? Reflecting on your interests can assist you in identifying areas that pique your interest and align with your values.

Consider your own strengths. What are your natural abilities, talents, and skills? What are you particularly talented at? Reflecting on your strengths can help you discover and leverage your unique capabilities in your entrepreneurial journey. Because they represent areas where you excel and feel confident, your strengths are frequently indicative of your passion.

Spend some time thinking about your interests and strengths. To gain a better understanding of yourself, consider journaling, talking to mentors or trusted friends, or using self-assessment tools. This reflection can help you discover your entrepreneurial purpose by providing insights into your areas of passion.

### Identifying Your Purpose and Mission

After considering your interests and strengths, the next step in discovering your passion is to determine your purpose and mission. Your purpose is the driving force behind everything you do as an entrepreneur. It is the driving force that fuels your motivation and gives your work meaning. Your mission is the specific aim or goal that you want to achieve through your business ventures.

To determine your purpose and mission, consider the following: What kind of change do you want to see in the world? What kind of impact do you want your company to have? What problem do you want to solve, or what need do you want to meet? Consider your entrepreneurial vision's values, beliefs, and personal experiences.

Consider the larger purpose and mission that align with your interests, passions, and strengths. Consider how you can use your skills, talents, and resources to make a positive difference in the world. You are more likely to be driven, focused, and committed to your entrepreneurial journey if you have a clear sense of purpose and mission.

## Turning Your Passion into a Business Idea

Once you've identified your passion, interests, strengths, purpose, and mission, the next step is to turn that passion into a viable business idea. Your passion can serve as the foundation for your business, but it must be translated into a concrete and viable concept capable of generating value for customers and meeting their needs in the long run.

Begin by conducting market research to identify potential opportunities that correspond to your passion and mission. Investigate market demand, competition, and trends in your desired industry. Look for gaps or unmet needs that your business idea can fill. This investigation can assist you in validating the viability and potential of your business idea.

Create a business plan outlining your vision, mission, target market, products or services, pricing strategy, marketing plan, and financial projections. Your business plan serves as a road map for your entrepreneurial journey and gives your business idea a clear direction. It can also be used to obtain funding or support from investors, partners, or stakeholders.

When turning your passion into a business idea, make sure there is a market need for your offering and that you have a clear plan for meeting that need. Passion alone will not sustain a successful business; it must be supported by a strong business strategy, market research, and financial planning.

Take the necessary steps to bring your business idea to life once you've created a business plan. Securing funding, establishing your legal and financial infrastructure, developing your products or services, developing your brand identity, and developing your marketing strategy may all be part of this process. Surround yourself with mentors, advisors, and a supportive network to help you along the way.

Remember that turning your hobby into a profitable business takes time, effort, and perseverance. It's critical to be realistic about potential challenges and uncertainties, and to be willing to adapt and pivot as needed. When you are truly enthusiastic about your business idea, it can fuel your determination and drive to overcome obstacles and achieve success.

Finally, discovering your passion is a critical step toward realizing your full potential as an entrepreneur. You can set yourself up for entrepreneurial success by reflecting on your interests and strengths, identifying your purpose and mission, and turning your passion into a viable business idea. Remember to conduct extensive market research, create a solid business plan, and be ready to adapt and persevere on your entrepreneurial journey. With passion as your driving force, you can realize your full potential and build a business that not only succeeds but also has a positive impact on the world.

## Chapter 2 Takeaways

1.  Examine your interests and strengths to discover your entrepreneurial passion.

2.  Determine your purpose and mission in order to connect your passion to a larger vision.

3.  Conduct market research to ensure that your business idea is viable.

4.  Create a detailed business plan outlining your vision, mission, and strategies.

5.  Surround yourself with mentors and a supportive network to help you along the way.

6.  Be realistic about the risks and challenges of entrepreneurship, and be willing to adapt.

7.  Using passion as your driving force, you can realize your full potential and build a successful business that has a positive impact.

# Chapter 3

# Building A Growth Mindset

As an entrepreneur, your mindset is essential to realizing your full potential for success. Your entrepreneurial journey can be greatly influenced by how you think, perceive challenges, and approach opportunities. In this chapter, we'll look at the power of mindset in entrepreneurship and how you can cultivate a growth mindset to overcome limiting beliefs and self-doubt while also achieving continuous learning and improvement.

## Understanding the Power of Mindset in Entrepreneurship

The set of beliefs, attitudes, and perspectives that shape how you perceive and interpret the world around you is referred to as your mindset. It has an impact on your thoughts, emotions, and behaviors, as well as the outcomes you achieve in your life and business. Mindset is critical in determining your ability to overcome challenges, adapt to change, take risks, and pursue opportunities in the context of entrepreneurship.

Having the right mindset is critical for business success. It is not only important to have a positive attitude or to be optimistic, but it is also important to cultivate a growth mindset that allows you to overcome obstacles, learn from failures, and continuously improve. A growth mindset is defined by the belief that your abilities and intelligence can be developed through hard work, perseverance, and education. This mindset promotes resilience, innovation, and a willingness to venture outside of one's comfort zone.

## Overcoming Self-Doubt and Limiting Beliefs

Overcoming limiting beliefs and self-doubt is one of the most difficult challenges that entrepreneurs face when developing a growth mindset. Limiting beliefs are negative thoughts or beliefs that prevent you from acting or achieving your goals. They can stem from a variety of sources, including past experiences, societal norms, or a fear of failure. Self-doubt, on the other hand, is characterized by a lack of confidence in one's abilities or the fear of not being good enough.

It is critical to identify and challenge your limiting beliefs and self-doubt in order to develop a growth mindset. Begin by becoming aware of the thoughts and beliefs that may be impeding your progress. Consider whether they are founded on facts or assumptions. Are they assisting or impeding your progress? Are they in line with your goals and values? Take deliberate steps to challenge and reframe your limiting beliefs and self-doubt once you've identified them. Positive affirmations and constructive self-talk should be used to replace negative thoughts. Surround yourself with people who will encourage and motivate you. Practice self-compassion and celebrate your accomplishments, no matter how minor they may appear. Remember that overcoming limiting beliefs and self-doubt is an ongoing process that necessitates conscious effort and practice.

## Cultivating a Growth Mindset for Continuous Learning and Improvement

A growth mindset is something you can cultivate and develop over time, rather than something you are born with. Adopting attitudes and behaviors that promote continuous learning, improvement, and resilience are part of cultivating a growth mindset.

1. **View challenges and failures as opportunities for growth and learning:** Rather than avoiding challenges or viewing failures as setbacks, consider them valuable experiences that provide insights, feedback, and opportunities for improvement. Adopt a "fail forward" mindset in which you learn from your mistakes and use them as stepping stones to success.

2. **Be open to learning and acquiring new skills:** As an entrepreneur, it is critical to be curious and open to learning. Maintain an awareness of industry trends, solicit feedback from mentors and advisors, participate in workshops or training programs, and invest in your personal and professional development. Expand your knowledge and skills on a regular basis to stay relevant and competitive in the ever-changing business landscape.

3. **Develop resilience and perseverance:** Entrepreneurship is not always easy; it is fraught with challenges, setbacks, and uncertainties. Developing resilience and perseverance is critical for overcoming obstacles and failings. Develop a positive and resilient mindset that will allow you to recover from failures, setbacks, and disappointments. Self-reflection and self-awareness are important for understanding your emotions and reactions to challenges, as well as developing healthy coping mechanisms to effectively manage stress and setbacks.

4. **Adopt a positive attitude toward change:** Change is unavoidable in business, and it can be both exciting and difficult. Develop an adaptability and flexibility mindset, and be open to change as an opportunity for growth and innovation. Change should be viewed as an opportunity to learn new things, explore new possibilities, and adapt your strategies to meet changing market demands.

5. **Develop a "can-do" attitude:** Having faith in your abilities and a "can-do" attitude can have a significant impact on your mindset as an entrepreneur. Instead of dwelling on problems or limitations, cultivate a positive and optimistic mindset that focuses on possibilities, solutions, and opportunities. Cultivate a sense of self-efficacy, or belief in your ability to complete tasks and

achieve your goals, and use it as a motivator in your entrepreneurial journey.

6. **Exercise self-motivation and goal-setting skills:** Entrepreneurs must be self-motivated and have a clear vision. Set SMART (specific, measurable, achievable, relevant, and time-bound) goals that are consistent with your vision and values. Break down your goals into smaller, more manageable steps, and keep track of your progress on a regular basis. Celebrate your accomplishments and use them as motivation to keep going.

7. **Surround yourself with a positive support network:** Creating a supportive network of mentors, advisors, peers, and like-minded people can have a significant impact on your mindset as an entrepreneur. Surround yourself with people who believe in your abilities, offer constructive feedback, and provide support during difficult times. To gain valuable insights, perspectives, and guidance, connect with other entrepreneurs, join industry associations, attend networking events, and seek mentorship or coaching.

## Conclusion

Finally, developing a growth mindset is critical for realizing your full potential as an entrepreneur. Understanding the power of mindset in entrepreneurship entails overcoming limiting beliefs and self-doubt, as well as cultivating attitudes and behaviors that promote continuous learning, improvement, and resilience. By adopting a growth mindset, you can approach challenges with optimism, see failures as opportunities for growth, and continuously adapt and innovate in an ever-changing business landscape. Remember that cultivating a growth mindset is a lifelong endeavor that necessitates conscious effort, self-awareness, and practice. Embrace the power of mindset to realize your full potential as an unstoppable entrepreneur.

## Takeaways from Chapter Three

1. Mindset is an important aspect of entrepreneurship.
2. Overcome self-doubt and limiting beliefs.
3. Develop a growth mindset.
4. Exercise self-motivation and goal-setting skills.
5. Surround yourself with a positive support network.
6. Accept failure as a learning experience.
7. Increase your resilience and perseverance.

# Chapter 4

## Setting Clear Goals

Setting specific and measurable goals is a critical aspect of entrepreneurship. Goals act as a road map for your actions, decisions, and priorities in order to achieve your vision and desired outcomes. In this chapter, we'll look at the importance of goal-setting in entrepreneurship, how to create SMART (Specific, Measurable, Achievable, Relevant, Time-bound) goals, and how to create an action plan to help you achieve your goals.

**The Importance of Goal-Setting in Entrepreneurship**
Goal-setting is an essential process in entrepreneurship because it allows you to define your direction, stay focused, and track your progress. It gives you a sense of purpose, motivation, and accountability to keep you on track toward your goals. Setting specific goals allows you to:

a. **Define your vision:** Goals assist you in clarifying your vision by identifying what you want to achieve in your business and why it is important to you. They serve as a compass that guides your decision-making and strategic planning by providing a clear sense of direction and purpose.

b. **Maintain focus and motivation:** Setting goals keeps you motivated and focused on your priorities.

They act as a motivator, pushing you to take action, overcome obstacles, and stay focused on your goals even when faced with obstacles or distractions.

c. **Track progress and success:** Goals provide a measurable framework for assessing your progress and success. Setting specific and measurable goals allows you to track your performance, identify areas for improvement, and celebrate your accomplishments, giving you a sense of accomplishment and satisfaction.

d. **Foster accountability:** Goals foster accountability by setting targets and deadlines for yourself. This encourages you to own your actions, stay committed to your goals, and accept responsibility for your results.

## Creating SMART Goals

It is critical to create SMART goals, which are Specific, Measurable, Achievable, Relevant, and Time-bound, when setting goals. SMART goals increase the likelihood of success by providing clarity, focus, and structure to your goal-setting process. Let's take a closer look at each SMART goal component:

a. **Specific:** Goals should be clear and specific, stating precisely what you want to accomplish. Avoid goals that are vague or ambiguous and lack clarity or specificity, as they can lead to confusion and uncertainty. Ask yourself, "What exactly do I want to accomplish?" Why is it significant? What are the goal's key components or milestones?

b. **Measurable:** Goals must be measurable, which means they must include quantifiable criteria that allow you to track your progress and success. Measurable goals provide a tangible way to assess your performance and determine whether you have met your objectives. Consider how you will measure progress or success. What key indicators or metrics should be monitored?

c. **Achievable:** Your goals should be realistic and attainable, taking into account your resources, constraints, and capabilities. Goals that are too ambitious or unrealistic can lead to disappointment or frustration. Goals, on the other hand, should be challenging enough to motivate you and push you out of your comfort zone. Is this goal attainable given my current resources, skills, and constraints? What potential stumbling blocks or challenges might arise?

d. **Relevant:** Your goals should be relevant to your overall vision, values, and priorities. They should be meaningful and worthwhile, and they should serve a specific purpose in your entrepreneurial journey. Set goals that are relevant to your long-term vision or business objectives rather than goals that are not relevant or aligned with them. Consider whether this goal is relevant to your overall vision and business objectives. What are the implications for my values and priorities?

e. **Time-bound:** Goals should be time-bound to create a sense of urgency and accountability. Goals without a deadline may lack motivation and urgency, resulting in procrastination or delay. Set realistic timeframes for achieving your goals and make sure they are achievable within that timeframe. Consider when you want to achieve this goal. What is a reasonable completion date?

## Developing an Action Plan to Achieve Your Goals

After you've established your SMART goals, create an action plan outlining the steps, resources, and timelines required to achieve them. An action plan is a road map that guides your daily activities and ensures you are making progress toward your goals. Here are some essential steps in creating an effective action plan:

a. **Divide your goals into smaller, more manageable tasks:** Determine the specific tasks or actions required to accomplish each goal. Divide them into smaller, actionable steps that are simple to track and complete.

b. **Set priorities for your tasks:** Sort and prioritize your tasks according to their importance and urgency.

Concentrate on the most important tasks that are aligned with your goals and have the greatest impact on your business.

c. **Assign responsibilities:** Determine who will be in charge of each task and communicate the roles and responsibilities clearly to ensure accountability. Tasks should be assigned to team members or partners based on their skills and experience.

d. **Establish deadlines:** Set deadlines for each task to instill a sense of urgency and accountability. Set realistic deadlines that allow for flexibility and take into account potential delays or obstacles.

e. **Allocate resources:** Determine the resources needed to complete each task, such as time, money, and tools. Make sure you have the resources you need to carry out your action plan effectively.

f. **Track and monitor progress:** Track and monitor the progress of your action plan on a regular basis to ensure that you are making progress toward your goals. Update your plan as circumstances change or new information becomes available.

g. **Maintain adaptability:** As you progress and encounter new challenges or opportunities, be prepared to adjust your action plan. Stay adaptable and open to change, and be willing to revise your plan as needed to stay on track.

## Conclusion

Setting specific goals and creating an action plan are critical steps in realizing your full potential as an entrepreneur. You can stay focused, motivated, and accountable in your entrepreneurial journey by setting SMART goals that are aligned with your vision, values, and long-term objectives, and developing an action plan that outlines the steps, resources, and timelines required to achieve your goals. As your business evolves, review and update your goals and action plan on a regular basis, and remain adaptable to overcome challenges and seize opportunities along the way. Remember that you can become an unstoppable entrepreneur and achieve the success you desire if you have a clear vision, well-defined goals, and a strategic action plan.

## Takeaways from Chapter 4

1. Setting specific, measurable, achievable, relevant, and time-bound (SMART) goals is critical for entrepreneurship success.

2. SMART goals offer a structured approach to goal-setting, which increases the likelihood of success.

3. Consider your vision and long-term objectives to establish goals that are consistent with your overall business strategy.

4. Break your goals down into smaller, more manageable tasks to make them more attainable and trackable.

5. As your business grows, review and update your goals on a regular basis, and celebrate your accomplishments along the way.

6. Creating an action plan is critical for guiding your daily activities and ensuring progress toward your goals.

7. In your action plan, prioritize your tasks, assign responsibilities, set deadlines, allocate resources, and track progress.

8. Be adaptable and willing to revise your action plan as needed to overcome obstacles and stay on track to achieve your goals.

# Chapter 5

## Developing a Winning Business Plan

A well-written business plan is an essential tool for any entrepreneur seeking to build a successful company. It functions as a road map, guiding you through the various stages of your business's journey, from concept to execution. In this chapter, we will look at the key components of a business plan, the significance of conducting market research and analyzing the competition, and how to develop a solid business model and financial projections to support your entrepreneurial ventures.

## Understanding the Key Components of a Business Plan

A business plan typically includes several key components that outline the fundamental aspects of your company. These elements may differ depending on the nature and size of your business, but they generally include the following:

1. **Executive Summary:** This section provides an overview of your company, including its mission, vision, and goals. It serves as a summary of your entire business plan and should be brief but compelling, capturing the essence of your company.

2. **Company Description:** This section contains detailed information about your company, such as its legal

structure, location, history, and ownership. You can also highlight your company's unique selling proposition (USP) and explain how it stands out in the market.

3. **Market Analysis:** Conducting extensive market research to understand your target market, customer segments, industry trends, and competitive landscape is part of this section. It should demonstrate your understanding of the market and how your company fits into it.

4. **Products and Services:** Provide a detailed description of your products or services, including their features, benefits, pricing, and differentiation. Highlight how your offerings meet your target customers' needs and preferences.

5. **Marketing and Sales Strategies:** Describe your marketing and sales strategies for attracting and keeping customers. Include your marketing strategies, advertising plans, distribution channels, and customer acquisition strategies.

6. **Organization and Management:** Describe your company's organizational structure, management team, and key personnel. Highlight their relevant skills, experience, and qualifications to your company.

7. **Financial Projections:** Include income statements, balance sheets, cash flow statements, and sales forecasts in your financial projections. These projections should

be based on reasonable assumptions and demonstrate your company's financial viability and sustainability.

8. **Funding Requirements:** If your business requires external funding, outline your funding needs, including the amount, purpose, and terms of the funding. Also, include information about your funding sources, such as investors, loans, or grants.

9. **Appendix:** Include any additional information in the appendix section, such as market research data, product prototypes, patents, licenses, or other relevant documents.

## Conducting Market Research and Analyzing the Competition

Market research is an important part of any business plan because it provides information about market dynamics, customer preferences, and competition. You can make informed decisions about your business strategy, marketing efforts, and product/service offerings if you understand the market and competition. The following are some essential steps for conducting effective market research:

1. **Determine your target market:** Define your target market clearly, including demographics, psychographics, behaviors, and customer needs. This will allow you to better tailor your products/services and marketing strategies.

2. **Gather data:** Compile relevant data from a variety of sources, including market reports, industry publications, government data, customer surveys, and focus groups. To gain a comprehensive understanding of the market and competition, use both primary and secondary data.

3. **Competitors' Analysis**: Examine your competitors' strengths and weaknesses, market share, pricing, distribution channels, and marketing strategies. Analyze their products/services, customer feedback, and reviews to identify gaps and opportunities for your company.

4. **The SWOT analysis:** Conduct a SWOT (Strengths, Weaknesses, Opportunities, and Threats) analysis to evaluate your company's internal strengths and weaknesses, as well as external market opportunities and threats. This analysis will assist you in identifying areas where you can capitalize on your strengths, address your weaknesses, capitalize on opportunities, and mitigate potential threats.

5. **Customer feedback:** Gather feedback from potential customers via surveys, focus groups, or other methods in order to understand their preferences, pain points, and expectations. This will allow you to better serve your target customers by fine-tuning your product/service offerings and marketing strategies.

6. **Developing a Solid Business Model and Financial Projections:** A solid business model and financial projections are essential components of a business plan because they demonstrate your company's financial viability and sustainability. When developing your business model and financial projections, keep the following points in mind:

a. **Business model:** Select a business model that corresponds to your products/services, target market, and revenue streams. B2B (Business-to-Business), B2C (Business-to-Consumer), subscription, freemium, e-commerce, and other business models are common. In your business plan, clearly outline your revenue sources, cost structure, pricing strategy, and sales channels.

b. **Financial projections:** Based on your market research, industry benchmarks, and assumptions, create realistic financial projections. Include projected income and balance sheets, as well as cash flow statements, for the next three to five years. Consider sales growth, expenses, gross margin, net profit, cash flow, and a break-even analysis. Your financial projections should demonstrate your company's financial viability and be supported by credible data and assumptions.

c. **Sensitivity analysis:** Use sensitivity analysis to determine how different scenarios will affect your financial projections. This will assist you in understanding the risks and uncertainties associated with your business and allowing you to make informed decisions about pricing, sales volumes, expenses, and other factors that may affect your financial performance.

d. **Funding requirements:** In your business plan, clearly outline your funding requirements, including the amount, purpose, and terms of the funding. If you intend to seek external funding, such as loans or investments, explain in detail how the funds will be used, how they will contribute to the growth of your business, and how you intend to repay or provide a return on investment (ROI) to your investors.

## Conclusion

Creating a winning business plan is an essential step for any entrepreneur seeking to build a successful company. Understanding the market and competition, developing a solid business model, and developing realistic financial projections are all necessary components. You can create a comprehensive and effective business plan that will serve as a roadmap for your entrepreneurial journey if you follow the key takeaways discussed in this chapter. Remember to conduct extensive market research in order to comprehend your target market, analyze the competition, and identify external opportunities and threats. Use this knowledge to create a business model that aligns with your products/services, target market, and revenue streams, as well as realistic financial projections that demonstrate your company's financial viability. Conduct sensitivity analysis to assess risks and uncertainties, and clearly outline your funding needs if applicable.

You will be better equipped to make informed decisions, allocate resources effectively, and navigate the challenges and opportunities that come with entrepreneurship if you have a well-crafted business plan in hand. Your business plan will be a guiding document that will assist you in staying focused on your goals, communicating your vision to stakeholders, and securing funding or investment if necessary.

Remember that a business plan is a living document that should be reviewed and updated on a regular basis as your company grows. Maintain your agility and adaptability, and be willing to refine and adjust your business plan as you gain market insights, feedback, and experience.

To summarize, creating a winning business plan is a critical step in realizing your full potential as an entrepreneur. It will give you a road map, assist you in making informed decisions, and lay a solid foundation for your business. You will be well-prepared to navigate the complexities of the business world and create a thriving and unstoppable entrepreneurial venture if you understand the key components of a business plan, conduct thorough market research, develop a solid business model, and develop realistic financial projections.

## Takeaways for Chapter 5

1. Any entrepreneur seeking to build a successful business must have a well-crafted business plan. It functions as a road map, guiding you through the various stages of your business journey and assisting you in making informed decisions.

2. Thorough market research and competitor analysis are critical for understanding your target market, customer preferences, industry trends, and competition. This knowledge will assist you in tailoring your business strategy, marketing efforts, and product/service offerings to meet your customers' needs and gain a competitive advantage.

3. Creating a solid business model and financial projections is critical for demonstrating your company's financial viability and sustainability. Your business model should be consistent with your products/services, target market, and revenue streams, and your financial projections should be supported by credible data.

4. Sensitivity analysis is critical for assessing the risks and uncertainties associated with your business and

comprehending the impact of various scenarios on financial performance. It will assist you in making informed decisions and reducing potential risks.

5. It is critical to clearly outline your funding requirements in your business plan, if applicable, in order to attract external funding and support your company's growth. Give a detailed explanation of how the funds will be used, how they will contribute to your company's success, and how you intend to repay or return your investors' money.

# Chapter 6

## Building a Strong Personal Brand

In today's competitive business landscape, building a strong personal brand is crucial for the success of entrepreneurs. Your personal brand is a reflection of your unique identity, values, skills, and expertise, and it sets you apart from others in the market. In Chapter 6 of "The Unstoppable Entrepreneur: Unlocking Your Full Potential for Success," we will explore the importance of personal branding, how to define your personal brand and unique selling proposition, establish an online presence through social media and personal branding, and leverage your personal brand to attract customers and partners.

## Defining Your Personal Brand and Unique Selling Proposition

Your personal brand is what distinguishes you from the competition and defines your unique value proposition. It includes your abilities, knowledge, experience, values, and personality. Personal branding necessitates introspection and self-awareness. You must identify your strengths, passions, and distinguishing characteristics that set you apart in your industry or niche.

### Ask yourself questions such as:

**a.** What are your core strengths and skills?

**b.** What are your unique experiences and qualifications?

**c.** What values and beliefs do you stand for?

**d.** What makes you different from others in your industry?

**e.** What problems do you solve for your customers?

By answering these questions, you can start crafting your personal brand and unique selling proposition. Your unique selling proposition (USP) is the unique value or benefit that you bring to your customers or partners. It should clearly communicate what sets you apart and why people should choose you over others.

## Establishing an Online Presence through Social Media and Personal Branding

Establishing an online presence is critical for developing a strong personal brand in today's digital age. Social media platforms provide powerful tools for showcasing your expertise, connecting with your target audience, and growing a community of devoted followers. In this section, we'll look at how to use social media and personal branding to build a strong online presence.

**a. Select the Appropriate Social Media Platforms**: Not all social media platforms are created equal, and not all of them are relevant to your personal brand. Determine which platforms your target audience uses and concentrate your efforts on those platforms.

LinkedIn, Twitter, Facebook, Instagram, and YouTube are all popular platforms for personal branding.

b. **Optimize Your Social Media Profiles**: Think of your social media profiles as virtual business cards. Optimize them to reflect your unique selling proposition and personal brand. Use professional photographs, write a compelling and succinct bio, and emphasize your skills, experience, and accomplishments.

c. **Share High-Quality Content:** In the world of social media, content is king. Create and distribute high-quality content that is both relevant to your target audience and consistent with your personal brand. This could include articles, videos, infographics, podcasts, and other formats that demonstrate your expertise while also adding value to your audience.

d. **Interact with Your Audience:** Social media is not a one-way street. Respond to comments, messages, and mentions to engage your audience. Develop relationships, add value, and position yourself as an authority in your field.

e. **Develop Relationships and Collaborate:** Social media can also be used to develop relationships and collaborate with influencers, potential customers, and partners. To increase your reach and opportunities, network strategically, collaborate with others in your industry, and leverage your personal brand.

## Leveraging Your Personal Brand to Attract Customers and Partners

A strong personal brand can lead to new opportunities, customers, and partnerships. In this section, we'll look at how you can use your personal brand to help your business grow.

a. **Increase Trust and Credibility:** Your personal brand is a reflection of your expertise, experience, and values, and it can aid in the development of trust and credibility with your target audience. People are more likely to trust your products or services and become customers if they perceive you as an authority in your niche.

b. **Establish Thought Leadership:** Developing a strong personal brand can position you as an industry thought leader. You can establish yourself as a go-to resource in your niche by consistently sharing valuable and insightful content, engaging with your audience, and showcasing your expertise. Customers, as well as potential partners, investors, and collaborators, may be attracted as a result of this.

c. **Attract Ideal Customers:** Your personal brand can also assist you in attracting ideal customers. When your personal brand aligns with your target audience's values and preferences, they are more likely to resonate with your message and be drawn to your products or services. Your personal brand can set you apart from the competition and make you the preferred option for your target audience. Personal branding can also help you build strong partnerships with other entrepreneurs, influencers, and industry leaders. When you have a strong personal brand, it can lead to opportunities for collaboration, joint ventures, and partnerships that benefit both parties. Your personal brand can be a powerful tool for networking and making meaningful connections with others in your industry.

d. **Increase Your Visibility and Opportunities:** A strong personal brand can help you gain visibility in your industry and open up new doors. You may be invited to speak at industry events, participate in interviews, guest post on blogs, or contribute to media outlets as you establish yourself as an authority and thought leader. These opportunities can assist you in broadening your reach, increasing your exposure, and attracting more customers and partners.

## Conclusion

To summarize, developing a strong personal brand is critical for any entrepreneur seeking to stand out in today's crowded marketplace. You can lay a solid foundation for success by defining your personal brand and unique selling proposition. It is also critical to establish a strong online presence through personal branding and social media, which can help you reach a larger audience and develop valuable relationships with customers and partners.

Finally, a compelling personal brand can help you distinguish yourself from competitors and establish yourself as an industry thought leader. This can help you attract ideal customers, form strong partnerships, raise your visibility, and discover new avenues for success on your entrepreneurial journey. As we continue on our entrepreneurial journey, let us remember the importance of developing a strong personal brand and the numerous benefits it can provide.

## Chapter 6 Takeaways

1. Building a strong personal brand is crucial for the success of entrepreneurs in today's competitive business landscape.
2. Defining your personal brand and unique selling proposition requires introspection and self-awareness to identify your strengths, passions, and unique qualities.
3. Establishing an online presence through social media and personal branding can help you showcase your expertise, connect with your target audience, and build a community of loyal followers.

4.  Leveraging your personal brand can attract customers, build partnerships, increase your visibility, and open up new opportunities.

5.  Consistently sharing valuable and relevant content, engaging with your audience, and showcasing your expertise can establish you as a thought leader in your industry and build trust and credibility with your target audience.

6.  Building a strong personal brand requires consistency, authenticity, and a clear alignment between your personal values and your target audience's preferences.

# Chapter 7

## Mastering Time Management

Time management is an essential skill for entrepreneurs who want to reach their full potential. Time is a valuable resource in today's fast-paced business world, and how you manage it can have a significant impact on your productivity, success, and overall well-being. In this chapter of "The Unstoppable Entrepreneur: Unlocking Your Full Potential for Success," we will look at how to manage your time effectively as an entrepreneur, how to prioritize tasks and maximize productivity, and how to balance work, personal life, and self-care for long-term success.

### The Importance of Effective Time Management for Entrepreneurs

Entrepreneurs must manage their time for a variety of reasons. To begin, as an entrepreneur, you are responsible for a variety of tasks and wear many hats, ranging from managing your business operations to marketing, sales, and customer service, among other things. Effective time management enables you to prioritize tasks, wisely allocate your time, and concentrate on the most important and high-impact activities that propel your business forward.

Second, time management prevents burnout and overwhelm. Entrepreneurship can be demanding and stressful, and if you don't manage your time well, you may find yourself working long hours, feeling overwhelmed, and experiencing a drop in productivity and overall well-being. Mastering time management techniques can help you achieve a better work-life balance, reduce stress, and achieve long-term success.

Finally, good time management enables you to make the best use of your time and resources. Time is a limited resource that can never be replenished. As an entrepreneur, it is critical to manage your time wisely and make the most of every minute in order to achieve your business objectives, fulfill your vision, and achieve the success you desire.

## Techniques for Prioritizing Tasks and Maximizing Productivity

a. **Establish Clear Goals and Priorities:** Establishing clear goals and priorities is the first step in effective time management. Define your short- and long-term objectives, as well as the tasks and activities that are most important and aligned with your business objectives. Prioritize your tasks according to their importance and urgency, and devote your time and energy to high-impact activities that produce results.

b. **Plan and Organize:** Effective time management requires planning and organization. Make a daily, weekly, and monthly schedule, and use tools like calendars, to-do lists, and productivity apps to help you stay on top of your tasks and deadlines. Divide your goals and tasks into smaller, more manageable steps and schedule them in your calendar to ensure they are completed on time.

c. **Delegate and Outsource:** As an entrepreneur, you must accept that you cannot do everything on your own. Delegate or outsource tasks that are not within your core competency to team members. This enables you to concentrate on your strengths and the tasks that require your unique expertise, while leveraging the skills and abilities of others to complete tasks more efficiently.

d. **Use the Time-Blocking Technique:** Time-blocking is a technique in which specific time blocks are assigned to specific tasks or activities. You can, for example, schedule time to check and respond to emails, work on marketing initiatives, or brainstorm new ideas. This allows you to stay focused, avoid multitasking, and better manage your time.

e. **Follow the 80/20 Rule:** According to the 80/20 rule, also known as the Pareto Principle, 80% of your results come from 20% of your efforts. Identify and prioritize the tasks or activities that produce the most results or have the greatest impact on your business in your time management strategy. Focus on the tasks that add the most value and eliminate or reduce non-essential tasks that do not help you achieve your goals.

f. **Reduce Distractions:** Distractions can seriously undermine your productivity and time management efforts. Identify and eliminate or reduce workplace distractions, such as unnecessary notifications, social media, or other non-essential tasks. Make your work environment conducive and focused so that you can focus on your tasks without interruptions.

g. **Use Productivity Techniques:** There are a variety of productivity techniques you can use to effectively manage your time. The Pomodoro Technique, which involves working in focused bursts of time followed by short breaks, and the Two-Minute Rule, which suggests tackling tasks that take less than two minutes to complete immediately rather than putting them off, are two popular techniques. Investigate various productivity techniques to determine which ones work best for you.

## Balancing Work, Personal Life, and Self-Care for Sustainable Success

To ensure long-term success as an entrepreneur, you must strike a balance between your work, personal life, and self-care. Neglecting your personal life and well-being can result in burnout, reduced productivity, and even health problems. Here are some helpful hints for striking a balance:

a. **Establish Boundaries:** Set clear boundaries between your professional and personal lives. Define work and non-work hours and adhere to them as much as possible. Avoid checking emails or working during personal time, and instead prioritize self-care activities like exercise, hobbies, and spending time with loved ones.

b. **Exercise Self-Care:** It is critical for your overall success as an entrepreneur to take care of your physical, mental, and emotional well-being. Make self-care a priority by getting enough sleep, eating healthy, and doing things that will recharge and rejuvenate you. Remember that you are your company's most valuable asset, and taking care of yourself should be a non-negotiable part of your time management strategy.

c. **Learn to Say No:** As an entrepreneur, you may be bombarded with requests, opportunities, and time demands. It is critical to develop the ability to say no to non-essential tasks, projects, or commitments that do not align with your priorities or values. Take on only what you believe will benefit your business and your personal well-being.

d. **Delegate and Collaborate:** Delegating tasks to team members or collaborating with others can help you share the workload and relieve the stress of having to manage everything yourself. Surround yourself with a trustworthy and capable team, and learn to trust and empower them to assume responsibility. This not only allows you to better manage your time, but it also fosters a sense of teamwork and collaboration in your business.

e. **Practice Mindfulness:** Mindfulness is a practice that entails being fully engaged in the task at hand in the present moment, without being distracted by the past or the future. Mindfulness practice can help you improve your focus, reduce stress, and increase your productivity and time management skills. In order to stay centered and focused, incorporate mindfulness techniques such as deep breathing, meditation, or mindfulness exercises into your daily routine.

## Conclusion

To summarize, mastering time management is a critical skill for entrepreneurs who want to maximize their productivity, achieve their business goals, and stay healthy. You can realize your full potential as an unstoppable entrepreneur by implementing effective time management techniques and balancing work, personal life, and self-care.

## Chapter 7 Takeaways

1. Time management is crucial for entrepreneurs to achieve their full potential for success. It allows you to prioritize tasks, avoid burnout, make the most of your

time and resources, and achieve a better work-life balance.

2. Effective time management techniques include setting clear goals and priorities, planning and organizing, delegating and outsourcing, using time-blocking techniques, practicing the 80/20 rule, minimizing distractions, and using productivity techniques.

3. Balancing work, personal life, and self-care is essential for sustainable success. Set boundaries, practice self-care, learn to say no, delegate and collaborate, and practice mindfulness to achieve a healthy work-life balance.

# Chapter 8

## Developing Resilience and Grit

You will undoubtedly face numerous challenges and setbacks as an entrepreneur on your path to success. The ability to cultivate resilience and grit, as well as persevere in the face of adversity, is critical to your entrepreneurial success. In this chapter, we will look at the importance of resilience and grit in entrepreneurship, as well as how to cultivate these qualities and use failures as stepping stones to success.

In entrepreneurship, challenges and setbacks are unavoidable. Entrepreneurs frequently face roadblocks that can derail their plans and progress, ranging from financial obstacles and market fluctuations to unexpected competition and unforeseen circumstances. What distinguishes successful entrepreneurs is their ability to recover from failures and setbacks and keep moving forward with determination and perseverance.

The ability to adapt and recover from challenges, stress, or adversity is referred to as resilience. It is your mental and emotional toughness that allows you to persevere in the face of adversity. Grit, on the other hand, is the determination and passion to achieve long-term goals despite obstacles or failures. Resilience and grit go hand in hand, and cultivating these characteristics can help you navigate the ups and downs of entrepreneurship with resilience and determination.

## Importance of Resilience and Grit in Entrepreneurship

Entrepreneurs must be resilient and tenacious for several reasons:

1. **Overcoming Obstacles and Setbacks:** Entrepreneurship is inherently difficult, and setbacks are unavoidable. Whether it's a failed product launch, a financial loss, or a market setback, resilience and grit are essential in overcoming these obstacles. Resilience allows you to recover from failures, setbacks, and disappointments, whereas grit provides you with the determination and perseverance to keep going in the face of adversity.

2. **Managing Stress and Uncertainty:** With constant changes and uncertainties in the market, competition, and business environment, entrepreneurship can be stressful and uncertain. Resilience allows you to adapt to new situations, deal with challenges, and stay focused on your goals, which helps you manage stress and uncertainty. Even in the face of uncertainty and ambiguity, grit keeps you motivated and driven to pursue your long-term vision.

3. **Maintaining Motivation and Drive:** Entrepreneurship necessitates long-term effort and

dedication. Resilience and grit enable you to maintain motivation and drive even when things get tough. Grit gives you the passion and perseverance to stay committed to your goals despite challenges and obstacles, whereas resilience allows you to bounce back from failures and setbacks.

4. **Developing a Positive Mindset:** Resilience and grit can also assist you in developing a positive mindset, which is essential for entrepreneurial success. Resilience aids in the development of a "can-do" attitude in which failures are viewed as learning opportunities and setbacks as temporary obstacles. Even when faced with challenges and setbacks, grit helps you stay positive and focused on your long-term vision.

## Cultivating Resilience and Grit

The good news is that grit and resilience can be cultivated and developed over time. Here are some techniques for developing resilience and grit in your entrepreneurial journey:

1. **Foster a Growth Mindset:** Develop a growth mindset, which is the belief that you can learn, grow, and improve through hard work and experience. Develop a positive attitude toward failures, setbacks, and challenges by viewing them as opportunities for growth and learning. Rather than dwelling on mistakes

or setbacks, consider what you can learn from them and how you can improve.

2. **Practice Self-Care:** It is critical for resilience and grit to take care of your physical, mental, and emotional well-being. Make self-care a priority in your daily routine. Get enough sleep, eat healthily, exercise regularly, and engage in relaxing and recharging activities. Taking care of yourself physically, mentally, and emotionally will help you develop the resilience and grit required to face entrepreneurship's challenges and setbacks.

3. **Create Coping Strategies:** Determine healthy coping strategies that work for you in dealing with stress and adversity. This could include mindfulness, meditation, journaling, talking to a mentor or trusted friend, or seeking professional help when necessary. Coping strategies can help you navigate difficult situations and recover from setbacks with resilience.

4. **Have Realistic Expectations:** Entrepreneurship can be difficult, and setbacks are unavoidable. Setting realistic expectations and understanding that failures and setbacks are part of the entrepreneurial journey are critical. When things don't go as planned, don't be too hard on yourself. Instead, concentrate on learning from the experience and using it to grow and improve.

5. **Learn from Failures:** Failures are unavoidable in business, but how you handle them is critical. Rather than dwelling on failures or becoming discouraged by them, view them as stepping stones to success. Consider what went wrong, what you could have done differently, and what you can take away from the experience. Accept failure as a valuable learning experience that can help you become a better entrepreneur.

6. **Surround Yourself with Supportive People:** Having a network of mentors, advisors, peers, and friends who believe in you and your entrepreneurial journey can significantly boost your resilience and grit. Surround yourself with people who can offer advice, encouragement, and perspective during difficult times. When you need help or advice, don't be afraid to ask for it; it's a sign of strength, not weakness.

7. **Maintain Focus on Your Purpose and Vision:** Having a clear sense of purpose and vision for your entrepreneurial venture can provide you with the motivation and drive to persevere in the face of challenges and setbacks. Keep your long-term goals in mind and your vision in mind, even when faced with obstacles. Remember why you started your entrepreneurial journey in the first place and use that motivation to propel you forward.

THE UNSTOPPABLE ENTREPRENEUR: Unlocking Your Full Potential for Success

## Conclusion

To summarize, developing resilience and grit is critical for entrepreneurs to overcome challenges, setbacks, and failures, as well as to persevere in the face of adversity. You can develop the resilience and grit required to unlock your full potential as an unstoppable entrepreneur by cultivating a growth mindset, practicing self-care, developing coping strategies, setting realistic expectations, learning from failures, surrounding yourself with supportive people, and remaining focused on your purpose and vision. Failures, remember, are not the end of the world, but rather valuable opportunities for growth and learning. Continue to be resilient, persevere with grit, and progress toward your entrepreneurial goals.

## Chapter 8 Takeaways

1. Resilience and grit are crucial qualities for entrepreneurs to overcome challenges and setbacks, manage stress and uncertainty, sustain motivation, and build a positive mindset.

2. Resilience and grit can be cultivated through developing a growth mindset, practicing self-care, developing coping strategies, setting realistic expectations, learning from failures, surrounding yourself with supportive people, and staying focused on your purpose and vision.

3. Embrace failures as learning opportunities and use them as stepping stones to success. Reflect on what

went wrong, learn from the experience, and continue moving forward with determination and perseverance.

4. Building resilience and grit takes time and effort, but it's an investment in your entrepreneurial success. Stay committed to developing these qualities and be patient with yourself along the journey.

# Chapter 9

## Building a Winning Team

Entrepreneurship is a difficult and demanding journey that requires careful planning to succeed. The importance of forming a strong team is one that should not be overlooked. A strong and capable team can help you realize your vision, implement your business strategies, and overcome obstacles along the way. In this chapter, we will look at the importance of a strong team in entrepreneurship, as well as topics like hiring the right people, cultivating a positive work culture, and effective team leadership and motivation, all of which are critical components for achieving your business objectives.

A strong team is the foundation of any successful entrepreneurial venture. Your team members are invaluable allies who work with you to support your efforts and make your ideas a reality. A diverse team with complementary skills and expertise provides your company with a wealth of knowledge, creativity, and innovation. Each team member brings unique strengths and perspectives to the table, resulting in improved problem-solving, decision-making, and strategic planning. You can delegate tasks and responsibilities with the right team in place, allowing you to focus on your core strengths and strategic priorities.

A strong team also allows your company to grow and scale more quickly. Leveraging your capable team's skills, knowledge, and networks can help you expand your business, enter new markets, and pursue new opportunities. A supportive team can help you navigate difficult times, provide diverse perspectives, and offer solutions to overcome obstacles. A diverse set of perspectives and experiences fosters innovation and creativity, which drives business growth and success.

Building a winning team starts with carefully selecting individuals who share your vision, values, and goals. A cohesive and high-performing team requires cultural fit. Investing in your team members' training and development improves their skills, knowledge, and capabilities. It is critical to create a positive work environment for team motivation, engagement, and performance. As an entrepreneur and a leader, you play a critical role in fostering a positive work culture by setting the tone for your team.

After assembling the right team and cultivating a positive work culture, the next step is to effectively lead and motivate your team to achieve your business objectives. Giving feedback and recognition, empowering and delegating, encouraging collaboration and teamwork, and providing opportunities for growth are all important techniques for effective team leadership and motivation. We will delve deeper into these topics in the following sections to provide you with insights and strategies for building a winning team for your entrepreneurial venture.

## Understanding the Significance of a Strong Team in Entrepreneurship

You cannot achieve success as an entrepreneur on your own. Building a winning team is an essential component of realizing your full potential. A strong team can assist you in realizing your vision, executing your business strategies, and overcoming obstacles along the way. In this chapter, we will look at the importance of a strong team in entrepreneurship, as well as how to hire the right people, create a positive work environment, and effectively lead and motivate your team to achieve your business goals.

## The Importance of a Strong Team in Entrepreneurship

A strong team is the foundation of any successful entrepreneurial endeavor. Your team members will collaborate with you, support you, and assist you in bringing your ideas to life. Here are some of the main reasons why assembling a winning team is critical to your business's success:

1. **Complementary Skills and Expertise:** A diverse team with complementary skills and expertise can provide your company with a wealth of knowledge,

creativity, and innovation. Each team member brings their own set of skills and perspectives to the table, which can lead to more robust problem-solving, decision-making, and strategic planning.

2. **Increased Productivity and Efficiency:** With the right team in place, you can delegate tasks and responsibilities, freeing up your time to focus on your core competencies and strategic priorities. A well-functioning team can effectively collaborate, streamline processes, and boost productivity and efficiency in your business operations.

3. **Rapid Growth and Scaling:** A strong team can assist you in achieving rapid growth and scaling of your business. You can use a capable team's skills, knowledge, and networks to expand your business, enter new markets, and pursue new opportunities.

4. **Assistance During Difficulties and Setbacks:** Entrepreneurship can be difficult, and setbacks are unavoidable. A supportive team can assist you in navigating difficult times, providing different perspectives, and offering solutions to overcome obstacles.

5. **Creativity and Innovation:** A diverse team with diverse perspectives and experiences can foster innovation and creativity in your company. A collaborative and inclusive workplace encourages

team members to share ideas, challenge the status quo, and devise new solutions, resulting in business growth and success.

## Hiring the Right People and Building a Positive Work Culture

Putting together a winning team begins with hiring the right people who share your vision, values, and goals. Here are some important steps to take when hiring and creating a positive work culture:

1. **Define Your Team's Roles and Responsibilities:** Before hiring, clearly define each team member's roles and responsibilities based on your business needs. Consider the skills, experience, and expertise required for each role, and make certain that team members understand their responsibilities.

2. **Hire for Cultural Fit:** A cohesive and high-performing team requires cultural fit. Look for candidates who share your company's values, vision, and culture. In addition to their skills and qualifications, consider their attitude, work ethic, and interpersonal skills.

3. **Encourage Diversity and Inclusion:** Diversity and inclusion are critical for assembling a winning team. Accept differences in skills, backgrounds, perspectives, and experiences. A diverse team can provide your company with new ideas, creativity, and innovation.

4. **Adequate Training and Development:** Invest in your team members' training and development to improve their skills, knowledge, and capabilities. To foster a culture of continuous improvement, provide opportunities for professional development, mentorship, and ongoing learning.

5. **Foster a Positive Work Environment:** Fostering a positive work environment is essential for team motivation, engagement, and performance. Encourage an open communication, mutual respect, collaboration, and recognition culture. Encourage and provide regular feedback to team members to help them improve and grow.

6. **Lead by Example:** As an entrepreneur and leader, you play a critical role in fostering a positive workplace culture. Set the tone for your team by leading by example. Show the values and behaviors that you expect from your team members. Be approachable, supportive, and open in your communication. Show gratitude and recognition for their efforts and accomplishments. Your leadership style and actions will have an impact on the morale, motivation, and performance of the team.

## Effectively Leading and Motivating Your Team to Achieve Your Business Goals

After you've hired the right people and created a positive work environment, the next step is to effectively lead and motivate your team to meet your business objectives. Here are some key techniques for effective team motivation and leadership:

1. **Communicate Expectations Clearly:** Establish clear expectations for your team members regarding their roles, responsibilities, and performance standards. Communicate your company's goals, objectives, and expectations clearly. Ensure that everyone understands your company's vision, mission, and values.

2. **Provide Feedback and Recognition:** Give your team members regular feedback on their performance. Recognize and appreciate their efforts, accomplishments, and contributions. Feedback and recognition help team members understand how they are performing and motivate them to keep working toward the business goals.

3. **Empower and Delegate:** Assign tasks and responsibilities to team members so that they can take ownership of their work. Trust their abilities and provide them with the resources and support they need to do their jobs well. Allow them to bring their unique strengths and perspectives to their work rather than micromanaging them.

4. **Encourage Collaboration and Teamwork:** Encourage your team members to collaborate and work together. Create an environment of mutual

support, respect, and cooperation. Create opportunities for team members to collaborate, share ideas, and solve problems as a group. Collaboration can improve creativity, innovation, and decision-making.

5. **Provide Opportunities for Growth:** Provide opportunities for your team members to advance their careers within your company. Provide training, mentoring, and coaching to aid in the development of new skills, knowledge, and abilities. Support their professional development and advancement, which will increase their motivation and commitment to the company.

6. **Lead with Empathy and Emotional Intelligence:** Demonstrate empathy for your team members and emotional intelligence in your leadership style. Recognize their wants, concerns, and difficulties. Be encouraging and compassionate. Build trusting, respectful, and understanding relationships with your team members.

7. **Effectively Handle Conflicts:** Conflicts are unavoidable in any team environment. It is critical for a leader to handle conflicts effectively and in a timely manner. Address conflicts as soon as possible, listen to all parties involved, and find fair and reasonable solutions. Unresolved conflicts can harm team

morale, productivity, and, ultimately, the success of your company.

8. **Celebrate Successes:** Commemorate your team's successes, milestones, and achievements. Recognize and appreciate their efforts and dedication. Celebrating accomplishments improves team morale, motivation, and engagement. It also promotes a positive work environment and encourages continued success.

## Conclusion

To summarize, assembling a winning team is a critical component of achieving entrepreneurial success. A strong team can help your company reach its full potential and achieve its objectives. You can create a high-performing team that is aligned with your business vision and mission by hiring the right people, creating a positive work culture, and effectively leading and motivating your team. Remember to communicate clearly, to give feedback and acknowledgement, to empower team members, to foster collaboration, and to lead with empathy and emotional intelligence. Celebrate successes, recognize team efforts, and invest in their ongoing growth and development. With the help of a winning team, you can overcome obstacles, capitalize on opportunities, and achieve unrivaled success as an unstoppable entrepreneur.

## Chapter 9 Takeaways

1. A strong team is the backbone of entrepreneurial success, providing complementary skills, productivity, and support during challenges.

2. Hiring for cultural fit, fostering diversity and inclusion, and providing training and development are crucial for building a positive work culture.

3. Effective team leadership involves clear communication, feedback, empowerment, collaboration, and growth opportunities.

4. Leading with empathy, emotional intelligence, and conflict resolution skills are essential for effective team management.

5. Celebrating successes and acknowledging team efforts boosts morale, motivation, and engagement.

6. Building a strong team takes time, effort, and investment. It is essential to carefully select team members who align with your business values and goals, and provide them with the necessary resources and support to excel in their roles.

7. A positive work culture, characterized by mutual respect, cooperation, and collaboration, creates an environment where team members can thrive and contribute their best to the business.

8. Effective team leadership involves setting clear expectations, providing regular feedback and

recognition, empowering team members, and fostering a culture of continuous learning and growth.

9. Leading with empathy and emotional intelligence, and handling conflicts effectively, are critical skills for a leader to create a cohesive and motivated team.

10. Celebrating successes and milestones, and showing appreciation for team members' efforts, fosters team morale, motivation, and a sense of ownership in achieving the business goals.

# Chapter 10

## Embracing Innovation and Adaptability

With rapid changes in technology, consumer preferences, market dynamics, and global trends, the modern business landscape is constantly evolving. To stay ahead of the competition and seize new opportunities, entrepreneurs must embrace innovation and adaptability. In this chapter, we will look at the importance of adaptability and innovation in entrepreneurship, as well as strategies for navigating the rapidly changing business landscape and key takeaways to implement in your entrepreneurial journey.

### Navigating the rapidly changing business landscape

With new technologies, changing consumer behaviors, and shifting market trends, the business landscape is dynamic and ever-changing. To be a successful entrepreneur, you must stay informed about these changes and adapt your business strategies accordingly. Here are some tips for navigating the ever-changing business landscape:

a. **Stay informed:** Stay current on industry trends, consumer preferences, technological advancements, and global changes that may affect your business. To stay up to date on the latest developments, keep up with industry news, attend conferences, participate in relevant forums, and engage with industry influencers.

b. **Conduct market research regularly:** Conduct market research on a regular basis to better understand your target market's needs, preferences, and behaviors. Maintain contact with your customers via feedback, surveys, and market research in order to identify changing trends and adjust your business strategies accordingly.

c. **Foster an innovative culture:** Develop an organizational culture that promotes creativity, innovation, and experimentation. Encourage your team members to think about continuous improvement and learning, and encourage them to come up with new ideas, solutions, and strategies to stay ahead of the competition.

d. **Develop strategic alliances:** Work with other companies, industry partners, and experts to leverage their expertise, resources, and networks. Strategic alliances can help you stay current on industry trends, gain access to new markets, and capitalize on emerging opportunities.

e. **Be agile and flexible:** Approach business operations, processes, and strategies in an agile and flexible manner. Be ready to change course as needed in response to market changes, customer feedback, and emerging trends. To stay nimble and responsive to changing market dynamics, embrace flexibility and agility as core values in your business.

## Embracing innovation and staying ahead of the competition

Entrepreneurship thrives on innovation. It is the driving force behind the development of new products, services, business models, and customer experiences that disrupt markets, add value, and propel companies forward. Here are some strategies for embracing innovation and remaining competitive:

a. **Promote an innovative culture:** Make your workplace one that promotes creativity, experimentation, and risk-taking. Create an environment in which team members are encouraged to question the status quo, come up with new ideas, and innovate in their roles. To foster innovation at all levels of the organization, encourage cross-functional collaboration, knowledge sharing, and brainstorming sessions.

b. **Invest in research and development (R&D):** Set aside resources, time, and money for R&D activities. R&D can assist you in identifying new technologies, business models, and opportunities that can provide you with a competitive advantage in the market. Collaborate with external partners, universities, and research institutions to leverage their expertise and resources for R&D projects.

c. **Encourage innovation:** Encourage customer-centric innovation by listening to and understanding your customers' needs, pain points, and preferences. To identify opportunities for innovation, use customer feedback, surveys, and data analytics. Involve your customers in the product development process and work together to develop solutions that meet their needs and preferences. Customer-centric innovation can assist you in developing products and services that are more relevant, competitive, and market-driven.

d. **Encourage a mindset of continuous improvement and learning:** Adopt a mindset of continuous improvement and learning. Encourage your team members to improve their skills, knowledge, and expertise on a regular basis. Provide opportunities for professional development, training, and learning programs to help them grow professionally. Encourage and value feedback in a culture where mistakes are viewed as opportunities for learning and improvement. Continuous improvement can assist you in identifying areas of your business that require innovation and keeping you ahead of the competition.

e. **Adopt technology:** Technology is a major driver of innovation and can have a significant impact on your business. Keep abreast of technological advancements in your industry and look for ways to use them to improve your products, services, processes, and customer experiences. To gain a competitive advantage and stay ahead of the market, embrace automation, data analytics, artificial intelligence, and other emerging technologies.

## Adapting to market trends and seizing new opportunities

Market trends are constantly shifting, and it is critical for entrepreneurs to adapt to these shifts and seize new opportunities as they arise. Here are some strategies for responding to market trends and taking advantage of new opportunities:

a. **Keep an eye on market trends:** Keep up to date on market trends, customer preferences, and emerging opportunities. Keep an eye on your competitors, industry influencers, and market reports to spot trends that may affect your company. Gain insights into market trends by using data analytics, market research, and customer feedback, and then adapt your strategies accordingly.

b. **Be agile and flexible:** As previously stated, adapting to market trends requires being agile and flexible in your approach to business operations, processes, and strategies. Be prepared to change course, pivot, or make strategic shifts in response to market changes. Maintain your agility and responsiveness to market dynamics to ensure that you are well-positioned to capitalize on new opportunities as they arise.

c. **Capitalize on emerging opportunities:** When you spot a new market opportunity, act quickly to seize it. Have a strategy in place to capitalize on new opportunities, whether it's the launch of a new product, the expansion into a new market, or the exploration of a new business model. Be proactive and take calculated risks to position your company as a market leader.

d. **Foster an agile and adaptable culture:** Develop a culture within your organization that values agility and adaptability as core values. Encourage your team members to be adaptable, to be open to new ideas, and to be willing to change their strategies and approaches as needed. Create a culture that encourages and rewards experimentation, innovation, and adaptation.

e. **Form a diverse and inclusive team:** A diverse and inclusive team can bring a wide range of perspectives, ideas, and approaches to problem-solving, which can be beneficial in adapting to market trends and seizing new opportunities. Create a diverse team in terms of skills, experiences, backgrounds, and perspectives. Create an inclusive workplace culture in which everyone's voice is heard and diverse viewpoints are valued.

## Conclusion

In conclusion, entrepreneurs must embrace innovation and adaptability in order to navigate the rapidly changing business landscape, stay ahead of the competition, and seize new opportunities. Entrepreneurs can unlock their full potential for success as unstoppable entrepreneurs by staying informed about market trends, consumer preferences, and technological advancements, fostering an environment of innovation and agility, and being willing to adapt and change course as needed.

## Chapter 10 Takeaways

1. Embrace innovation as a driving force for creating value, disrupting markets, and staying ahead of the competition.
2. Foster a culture of innovation within your organization, invest in research and development, and involve customers in the innovation process.
3. Be agile and flexible in your approach to business operations, processes, and strategies, and be willing to adapt and change course as needed based on market changes and customer feedback.
4. Stay updated with the latest technological advancements in your industry and explore ways to

leverage them to improve your products, services, processes, and customer experiences.

5. Monitor market trends, be proactive in identifying emerging opportunities, and have a plan in place to capitalize on them.

6. Foster a culture of agility and adaptability within your organization, and build a diverse and inclusive team that can bring varied perspectives to problem-solving.

# Chapter 11

## Mastering Sales and Marketing

Sales and marketing are essential components of any successful business venture. To drive revenue, attract customers, and grow your business, you must master the art of selling and effectively promoting your products or services. We will look at key strategies for developing effective sales and marketing plans, understanding your target audience, creating compelling offers, and leveraging various marketing channels to achieve success as an unstoppable entrepreneur in this chapter.

### Understanding Your Target Audience

The foundation of any successful sales and marketing strategy is understanding your target audience. It is difficult to tailor your messaging, offers, and marketing efforts to resonate with your ideal customers unless you have a clear understanding of who they are. Begin by developing detailed buyer personas that represent your ideal customers' demographics, preferences, pain points, and purchasing behaviors. Conduct market research, analyze customer data, and solicit feedback to gain an understanding of their needs, motivations, and preferences.

You can create compelling offers that address your target audience's pain points and provide solutions to their problems once you have a clear understanding of them. Your products or services should be positioned as a solution to their needs and desires, and your messaging should clearly communicate the value they will receive if they choose your offerings. Remember to distinguish yourself from competitors and highlight what makes your company unique.

## Creating Compelling Offers

Making compelling offers is an important part of mastering sales and marketing. Your offers should entice your target audience and give them a compelling reason to choose your products or services. Begin by identifying your offerings' unique value proposition (UVP) - what makes them special, different, and better than the competition. Your UVP should be clear and concise, and it should communicate the benefits to your customers.

Create compelling messages that highlight the benefits of your offerings and elicit emotional responses from your target audience. Highlight how your products or services can help them solve problems, improve their lives, or fulfill their dreams. To build trust and credibility, use persuasive language, storytelling techniques, and social proof such as testimonials, case studies, or success stories. Remember to tailor your messages to different marketing channels and adapt them to your target audience's preferences and behaviors on each platform.

## Leveraging Various Marketing Channels

Entrepreneurs can use a variety of marketing channels to promote their products or services and reach their target audience. The options range from traditional channels like print, television, and radio to digital channels like social media, email marketing, content marketing, search engine optimization (SEO), pay-per-click (PPC) advertising, and influencer marketing.

To effectively leverage various marketing channels, it is critical to understand your target audience's preferences and behaviors on each platform. Conduct market research to determine which platforms your target audience prefers, their content consumption habits, and how they prefer to interact with brands. Develop a multi-channel marketing strategy based on this data, including a mix of channels that are most relevant to your audience and align with your business goals.

## Continuous Monitoring and Optimization

To ensure the effectiveness of your marketing efforts, you must regularly monitor and measure performance across all channels. You can improve your strategies by analyzing data and insights. This may entail testing various messaging, creative assets, targeting options, and call-to-actions to determine what resonates best with your audience and generates the highest return on investment (ROI).

## Consistent Brand Messaging

Developing consistent and compelling brand messaging is critical for establishing a strong brand identity. Your brand should have a distinct voice, tone, and identity that resonates with your target audience and distinguishes you from your competitors. Consistency in brand messaging helps to raise brand awareness, establish trust, and reinforce your value proposition in the minds of your customers.

## Power of Content Marketing

Content marketing is a powerful tool in your sales and marketing strategies. By creating high-quality, relevant, and valuable content, you can establish yourself as an industry authority, attract and engage your target audience, and drive organic traffic to your website. Blog posts, articles, videos, infographics, ebooks, webinars, and other forms of content marketing are examples. By providing valuable content that educates, inspires, and solves problems for your target audience, you can establish yourself as a trusted resource and build long-term relationships with your customers.

## Conclusion

Finally, effective marketing strategies necessitate a multifaceted approach that incorporates several key strategies. Understanding your target audience, creating compelling offers, and leveraging various marketing channels are critical for increasing your reach and engaging with your audience. Consistent brand messaging across all touch points builds trust and reinforces your brand's value proposition. Embracing content marketing, such as through high-quality, relevant, and valuable content, positions you as an industry authority and fosters long-term relationships with customers.

Building relationships through active engagement and personalized experiences creates brand advocates who can amplify your message and contribute to your success. Measuring results through data analysis and insights allows you to optimize your strategies based on real-time feedback. Staying adaptable and flexible in your marketing approach allows you to adapt to changing industry trends and consumer behaviors and seize new opportunities. Investing in long-term brand building rather than short-term tactics aids in the creation of a strong and memorable brand that can withstand the test of time.

Ultimately, remaining customer-centric and prioritizing your audience's needs and preferences should be at the heart of your marketing strategies. Understanding your audience, creating compelling offers, leveraging multiple marketing channels, maintaining consistent brand messaging, embracing content marketing, building relationships, measuring results, remaining adaptable, investing in long-term brand building, and remaining customer-centric can help you craft effective marketing strategies that drive growth, build brand equity, and foster long-term success for your business.

## Chapter 11 Takeaways

1. To effectively reach your target audience, create detailed buyer personas and conduct market research to understand their needs, preferences, and pain points, and then tailor your messaging and offers accordingly.

2. Craft compelling offers that highlight the unique value proposition (UVP) of your offerings, using persuasive language, storytelling, and social proof to create trust and credibility, in order to entice your target audience.

3. Develop a multi-channel marketing strategy that aligns with your business goals and includes platforms relevant to your audience, and continuously monitor and optimize your marketing efforts based on data and insights.

4. Establish a consistent brand identity, voice, and tone that resonates with your target audience, differentiates you from competitors, and builds brand awareness and trust through consistent brand messaging.

5. Leverage the power of content marketing by creating high-quality, relevant, and engaging content that addresses the needs and pain points of your target

audience, positioning your brand as a thought leader and authority in your industry.

6. Build genuine, long-term relationships with your audience through personalized and relevant interactions, using email marketing, social media, and other communication channels to engage, listen to feedback, and provide excellent customer service.

7. Continuously measure and analyze the performance of your marketing efforts using relevant metrics and data, to identify what's working and what's not, and make data-driven decisions to optimize your marketing strategies for better results.

8. Stay adaptable and agile in your marketing approach by staying updated with industry trends, consumer behavior, and technology advancements, and being willing to adapt and optimize your strategies accordingly.

9. Invest in long-term brand building strategies, being patient and consistent in delivering on your brand promise, providing exceptional customer experiences, and cultivating brand loyalty among your audience.

10. Always prioritize the needs, preferences, and satisfaction of your customers, listening to their feedback, addressing their concerns, and continuously improving your offerings based on their needs, to build

customer loyalty and advocacy, and drive long-term business success.

# Chapter 12

## Scaling Your Business for Long-term Success

Congratulations! You have successfully built your business from the ground up to a level of success that many entrepreneurs strive for. However, you are now ready to take your company to the next level, to scale it for long-term success. Scaling a business entails growing it sustainably, managing risks, overcoming obstacles, and leaving a legacy that will last. In this chapter, we'll look at how to scale your business, manage risks, and leave a legacy as an unstoppable entrepreneur.

### Strategies for Scaling Your Business Sustainably

Scaling a business necessitates meticulous planning and strategic execution. It is not only important to grow your business quickly, but also to do so sustainably to ensure its long-term success. Here are some key strategies for sustainable business growth:

a. **Establish Your Growth Objectives:** Before you begin scaling your business, you must first establish your growth objectives. What do you hope to achieve with your company? Do you want to increase your market share, diversify your product offerings, or expand geographically? Setting specific growth goals will allow you to better align your strategies and tactics.

b. **Create a Scalable Business Model:** Your current business model may have worked well in the beginning, but it may not be scalable for long-term growth. Consider how you can streamline processes, leverage technology, and automate repetitive tasks to support growth in your business model. A scalable business model will enable you to handle increased demand efficiently as your company grows.

c. **Create a High-Performance Team:** When it comes to scaling your business, your team is a critical asset. As your company expands, it is critical to attract and retain top talent who can help you execute your growth strategies. Create a strong leadership team, empower your employees, and provide them with the resources and training they need to succeed in their roles. A high-performing team will be critical in supporting your company as it grows.

d. **Concentrate on Customer Acquisition and Retention:** Getting and keeping customers is critical to growing your business. Invest in marketing and sales strategies that can effectively attract new customers while also retaining current ones. To foster loyalty and repeat business, provide excellent customer experiences, deliver value, and build strong relationships with your customers.

e. **Obtain Adequate Funding:** Scaling a business frequently necessitates the acquisition of additional capital to support increased operational costs, marketing efforts, and expansion plans. Investigate different funding options, such as equity financing, debt financing, or partnerships, to ensure you have enough capital to support your expansion plans.

f. **Leverage Technology and Innovation:** Technology and innovation can help you scale your business. Investigate how technology can help you optimize your business processes, increase efficiency, and expand into new markets. To stay ahead of the competition, embrace innovation and keep up with industry trends.

g. **Form Strategic Partnerships:** Strategic partnerships can provide valuable resources, expertise, and access to new markets, allowing your company to grow faster. Explore mutually beneficial collaborations with potential partners who share your business goals and can complement your offerings.

**Managing Risks and Overcoming Growth Challenges**

Scaling a business entails a number of risks and challenges. To ensure a smooth scaling process, it is critical to be prepared and manage these risks proactively. Here are some key considerations for risk management and growth challenges:

a. **Identify and Mitigate Risks:** Identify potential risks associated with scaling your business and devise mitigation strategies. Among the risks are increased competition, operational challenges, financial risks, and regulatory changes. Prepare contingency plans to address potential risks and reduce their impact on your business.

b. **Maintain Financial Health:** Growing a business necessitates careful financial management. Maintain a close eye on your finances, including cash flow, revenue, and expenses, and make sure you have a solid financial plan in place to support your growth goals. Consider the additional costs that may arise from scaling, such as hiring additional staff, expanding into new markets, and investing in technology. Implement effective financial controls and review and adjust your financial plan on a regular basis to ensure that your business remains financially healthy during the scaling process.

c. **Optimize Operations:** Scaling a business frequently necessitates changes to operational processes in order to accommodate increased demand. Evaluate your current operations and identify areas where you can improve efficiency and productivity. To support your growth plans, streamline processes, automate repetitive tasks, and implement scalable systems and tools. As your business grows, review and optimize your operations on a regular basis to ensure peak performance.

**d. Maintain a Strong Focus on Customer Experience:** As your business grows, it is critical to keep a strong focus on providing an exceptional customer experience. Your customers are the backbone of your company, and their satisfaction and loyalty are critical to your long-term success. Maintain a pulse on your customers' needs and preferences, and prioritize their satisfaction as you expand. Invest in customer service, collect feedback, and make changes as needed to continuously improve the customer experience.

**e. Manage Talent and Culture:** Growing a business often necessitates hiring more employees to support increased operations. To ensure that your team remains aligned with your company's values and goals, it's critical to carefully manage talent and culture during the scaling process. Hire top talent who fits your company culture and provides them with the resources and support they need to succeed in their roles. Develop a positive and welcoming workplace culture that encourages collaboration, innovation, and growth.

**f. Maintain Agility and Adapt to Change:** Scaling a business necessitates agility and the ability to adapt to market and business environment changes. Prepare to pivot and adjust your strategies as necessary to stay ahead of the competition and navigate any challenges that may arise. To scale your business sustainably, keep up with industry trends, monitor market changes, and be open to change and innovation.

## Creating a Legacy and Leaving a Lasting Impact as an Entrepreneur

As a business owner, you have the opportunity to leave a legacy and make a long-lasting impact. Here are some strategies to think about as you strive to leave a lasting legacy:

a. **Define Your Vision and Mission:** Creating a legacy for your business requires a clear vision and mission. Define your purpose and what you want your company to accomplish beyond financial success. Your vision and mission should reflect your values, goals, and desired global impact.

b. **Incorporate Social and Environmental Responsibility:** Consider incorporating social and environmental responsibility into your business practices. Adopt sustainable and ethical business practices that benefit society and the environment. This can include things like lowering your carbon footprint, supporting social causes, and volunteering in your community. Social and environmental responsibility can boost your brand's reputation and have a positive impact on the world.

c. **Inspire and Mentor Others:** As a successful entrepreneur, you have valuable knowledge and experience that you can use to motivate and inspire others. Share your knowledge and insights with aspiring entrepreneurs, peers in the industry, and your community. Mentorship can help others succeed and have a positive impact on the business world.

d. **Promote a Positive Organizational Culture:** Your organization's culture is critical to making a long-term impact. Create a culture that values diversity, inclusion, and innovation. Encourage your team members' collaboration, creativity, and lifelong learning. A positive organizational culture can attract and retain top talent, foster innovation, and foster a welcoming environment in which employees can thrive.

e. **Establish Strong Relationships with Stakeholders:** Establishing strong relationships with stakeholders such as customers, employees, investors, and partners is critical to leaving a lasting impression as an entrepreneur. Maintain these connections by being open, communicative, and trustworthy. Show genuine concern for your stakeholders' well-being and prioritize their interests. Strong relationships based on trust and mutual respect can lead to long-term collaborations, loyal customers, and a positive reputation that can outlast your company.

f. **Innovate and Adapt to Changing Needs:** In order to leave a lasting impression, it is critical to constantly innovate and adapt to changing customer needs and market dynamics. Stay ahead of the competition by investing in R&D, staying current on industry trends, and being open to new ideas and technologies. Adopt an innovative mindset and constantly evolve your business to meet the changing needs of your stakeholders.

g. **Plan for Succession:** Planning for succession is an important part of leaving a lasting legacy for your company. Create a succession plan to ensure that your business thrives even after you step away from it. Identify and develop potential successors, document your business processes and strategies, and build a strong leadership team capable of carrying out your vision and mission.

## Conclusion

Scaling your business for long-term success necessitates careful planning, execution, and ongoing adaptation. You can scale your business sustainably and leave a lasting impact as an entrepreneur by implementing effective risk management strategies, optimizing operations, focusing on the customer experience, and creating a positive organizational culture. To ensure that your business thrives beyond your entrepreneurial journey, embrace innovation, prioritize social and environmental responsibility, and plan for succession. Remember that an entrepreneur's journey is about more than just financial success; it is also about leaving a legacy that can positively impact the world.

## Chapter 12 Takeaways

1. Scaling a business requires strategic planning, effective execution, and careful management of resources to ensure sustainable growth.

2. Managing risks and challenges, such as financial considerations, operational efficiency, and talent management, is crucial during the scaling process.

3. Focus on delivering exceptional customer experience, maintaining a positive organizational culture, and incorporating social and environmental responsibility into your business practices to create a lasting impact.

4. Stay agile and adaptable to changes in the market and business environment to sustainably scale your business.

5. Plan for succession to ensure that your business continues to thrive beyond your entrepreneurial journey.

# Chapter 13

## Maintaining Work-Life Balance

It's easy as an entrepreneur to get caught up in the hustle and bustle of running a business and neglect your personal well-being. Maintaining a healthy work-life balance, on the other hand, is critical for long-term success because it can prevent burnout, boost productivity, and improve overall well-being. In this chapter, we will look at how to maintain a healthy work-life balance as an entrepreneur, how to manage stress, avoid burnout, and how to prioritize self-care for long-term success.

## Strategies for Maintaining a Healthy Work-Life Balance as an Entrepreneur

As an entrepreneur, you must devise strategies to help you maintain a healthy work-life balance. Consider the following key strategies:

a. **Establish Boundaries:** One of the difficulties of being an entrepreneur is that work can easily spill into personal time, particularly if you work from home or have flexible working hours. It is critical to distinguish between work and personal time. Define and communicate your working hours to your team, clients, and stakeholders. During personal time, avoid checking work-related emails or taking business calls.

Setting boundaries will assist you in keeping work and personal life separate, reducing the risk of burnout and maintaining a healthy balance.

b. **Delegate and Prioritize:** It's common for entrepreneurs to wear multiple hats and take on multiple responsibilities. However, it is critical to learn how to effectively delegate tasks and prioritize your time. Identify tasks that can be delegated or outsourced to your team, and concentrate on high-value activities that truly require your attention. You can avoid overwhelm and achieve a better work-life balance by delegating and prioritizing.

c. **Make a plan and stick to it:** Making a plan and sticking to it can help you stay organized and manage your time effectively. Make a plan that includes time for work, personal activities, and self-care. Set realistic goals and deadlines, and stick to your schedule to the greatest extent possible. Planning and scheduling can help you maintain a healthy work-life balance, reducing stress and increasing productivity.

d. **Learn to Say No:** As an entrepreneur, you will frequently face multiple demands on your time and energy. It is, however, critical to learn to say no when necessary. Avoid overcommitting and taking on too many tasks or projects, which may have a negative impact on your work-life balance. Learn to prioritize your time and energy by saying no to non-essential tasks or activities.

e. **Make Separate Spaces:** If you work from home, it's critical to separate work and personal activities. Create a separate office or workspace for work that is separate from your personal space. Having separate physical spaces can assist you in drawing a clear line between work and personal life, reducing the temptation to work outside of designated working hours.

## Stress Management and Avoiding Burnout

Because the demands of running a business can be overwhelming, entrepreneurs frequently face stress and burnout. However, in order to maintain a healthy work-life balance, it is critical to effectively manage stress and avoid burnout. Here are some tips for dealing with stress and avoiding burnout:

1. **Develop Self-Awareness:** Self-awareness is essential for stress management. Keep an eye on your thoughts, emotions, and physical sensations to spot early signs of stress or burnout. Recognize and validate your feelings, and then take the necessary steps to address them. Mindfulness techniques, such as meditation or deep breathing, can also help you effectively manage stress.

2. **Seek Help:** Having a support system in place can help you manage stress and avoid burnout. Seek help from friends, family, or trusted mentors. Surround yourself with positive and supportive people who can offer you encouragement, advice, and a different point of view. If necessary, do not be afraid to seek professional assistance, such as therapy or coaching.

3. **Take Rest Periods:** Taking frequent breaks throughout the day can assist you in managing stress and avoiding burnout. Schedule breaks into your workday and use them to do things that will help you relax and recharge. Walk, listen to music, or do yoga or stretching exercises. Taking breaks can assist you in reducing stress, increasing productivity, and maintaining a healthy work-life balance.

4. **Manage Your Time Effectively:** Effective time management can help you reduce stress and avoid burnout. Determine the most important tasks and prioritize them. To effectively manage your time and avoid multitasking, use tools and techniques such as the Pomodoro Technique. Avoid overburdening your schedule and be realistic about how much you can get done in a day.

## Putting Self-Care and Well-Being First for Long-Term Success

Prioritizing self-care and well-being as an entrepreneur is critical for long-term success. Here are some ideas for making self-care and well-being a priority:

1. **Exercise on a Regular Basis:** Regular exercise is essential for maintaining physical and mental well-being. Include regular exercise in your daily routine, whether it's going for a run, doing yoga, or attending a fitness class. Exercise can help you reduce stress, increase energy, and improve your overall well-being.

2. **Develop Healthy Habits:** Developing healthy habits such as eating a balanced diet, getting enough sleep, and avoiding harmful substances can assist you in maintaining optimal health and well-being. Get enough sleep, avoid smoking and excessive alcohol consumption, and avoid skipping meals or relying on processed foods.

3. **Pursue Hobbies and Interests:** Having interests and hobbies outside of work can help you maintain a healthy work-life balance and improve your overall well-being. Participate in activities that you enjoy, such as music, painting, or sports. Hobbies and interests can help you relieve stress, boost your creativity, and promote personal growth.

4. **Take some time off:** Taking time away from work is essential for achieving a healthy work-life balance and avoiding burnout. Plan regular vacations or breaks and use them to do things that will help you relax and recharge. Taking time away from work can help you reduce stress, improve your creativity, and promote your overall well-being.

## Conclusion

Entrepreneurs can maintain a healthy work-life balance, reduce stress, avoid burnout, and achieve long-term success by implementing these strategies and prioritizing self-care and well-being. Remember that self-care is not a luxury but a necessity for long-term success as an entrepreneur.

## Chapter 13 Takeaways

1. Maintaining a healthy work-life balance is crucial for long-term success as an entrepreneur.

2. Strategies for maintaining a healthy work-life balance include setting boundaries, delegating and prioritizing, planning and scheduling, learning to say no, and creating separate spaces.

3. Managing stress and avoiding burnout requires practicing self-awareness, seeking support, taking breaks, and practicing effective time management.

4. Prioritizing self-care and well-being requires engaging in regular exercise, practicing healthy habits, pursuing hobbies and interests, and taking time off.

# Chapter 14

## Giving Back and Paying It Forward

As an entrepreneur, success entails not only achieving personal and financial objectives, but also having a positive impact on your community and society. In this chapter, we'll look at the importance of social responsibility in entrepreneurship, how entrepreneurs can give back to their communities, and how to pay it forward to inspire the next generation of entrepreneurs.

## The Importance of Social Responsibility in Entrepreneurship

The ethical and moral obligations that individuals and organizations have to the well-being of society as a whole are referred to as social responsibility. Social responsibility in the context of entrepreneurship goes beyond simply maximizing profits and focuses on creating value for all stakeholders, including employees, customers, suppliers, investors, and the broader community.

Socially responsible entrepreneurship entails considering the social and environmental consequences of business decisions and taking actions that benefit society as a whole. It is about building a company that not only generates financial success, but also addresses societal issues and has a positive impact on the world.

Social responsibility is important in entrepreneurship for several reasons:

a. **Improves Reputation and Brand Image:** Being socially responsible can improve your company's reputation and brand image. Consumers and investors are increasingly looking for companies that are dedicated to making a positive impact on society and are willing to support and invest in such companies. You can build trust, loyalty, and goodwill among your stakeholders by demonstrating a strong sense of social responsibility, which will ultimately benefit your business in the long run.

b. **Promotes Innovation and Sustainability:** Social responsibility can promote business innovation and sustainability. You can identify new opportunities for innovation by considering the social and environmental impacts of your business operations, such as developing sustainable products or processes, reducing waste, and conserving resources. Adopting sustainable practices can also assist you in mitigating risks associated with environmental regulations and changing consumer preferences, as well as creating a more resilient and future-proof business.

c. **Promotes Employee Engagement and Retention:** Social responsibility has the potential to increase employee engagement and retention. Employees are more likely to be motivated and committed to a company that shares their values and works for the greater good. You can attract and retain top talent, boost employee morale and productivity, and foster a positive work culture by incorporating social responsibility into your business practices.

d. **Gives back to the community and society:** Entrepreneurs can use social responsibility to improve the well-being of their communities and society as a whole. Businesses can have a significant impact on local economies by creating jobs, supporting local initiatives, and addressing societal issues like poverty, inequality, and environmental degradation. Entrepreneurs can help to create a more inclusive and sustainable society by giving back to the community.

## Making a Positive Impact on Your Community and Society

As an entrepreneur, you can have a positive impact on your community and society in a variety of ways. Here are some ideas for how to give back and make a difference:

1. **Corporate Social Responsibility (CSR):** Putting in place a formal CSR program can be a powerful way to give back to your community and society. Integrating social and environmental concerns into your business operations and decision-making

processes is what CSR is all about. This can include charitable donations, volunteering, environmental conservation, and social initiatives that are consistent with your company's values and goals.

2. **Philanthropy:** Participating in philanthropic activities can be an effective way to make a positive difference in society. Donating money, resources, or expertise to charitable organizations, non-profits, or community projects that align with your values and priorities can be part of this. Philanthropy allows you to contribute to positive change in your community or beyond by supporting causes that are important to you.

3. **Corporate Social Entrepreneurship:** Another way to make a difference is through corporate social entrepreneurship, which entails developing innovative business models that address societal challenges while also making a profit.

4. **Employee Volunteering and Engagement:** Encouraging and supporting employee volunteering and engagement can be an effective way to make a difference in your community. Allowing employees to volunteer their time and skills for charitable organizations or community projects can help employees feel a sense of purpose and fulfillment while also benefiting the community.

5. **Collaborations and Partnerships:** Working with other businesses, organizations, or stakeholders to address societal challenges can multiply your impact and create synergies. Strategic partnerships, joint ventures, and collaborations allow you to pool resources, expertise, and networks to effect more significant and long-term change. Collaboration with local non-profit organizations or government agencies, for example, can help you better leverage their knowledge and resources to address community needs.

6. **Environmental Sustainability:** Dealing with environmental issues is an important aspect of social responsibility. Implementing sustainable practices in your business operations, such as lowering your carbon footprint, conserving resources, reducing waste, and promoting eco-friendly products or services, can all help to protect and preserve the environment. By promoting sustainability and addressing environmental issues, this can have a positive impact on the community and society.

## Paying It Forward and Inspiring the Next Generation of Entrepreneurs

One of the most powerful ways to give back and make a lasting impact as an entrepreneur is by paying it forward and inspiring the next generation of entrepreneurs. By sharing your knowledge, experiences, and resources, you can help aspiring entrepreneurs overcome challenges, learn from your successes and failures, and build a foundation for their own entrepreneurial journey.

Here are some strategies for paying it forward and inspiring the next generation of entrepreneurs:

1. **Mentoring and Coaching:** Mentoring and coaching aspiring entrepreneurs can be a meaningful way to share your knowledge, skills, and experiences. You can offer guidance, advice, and support to help them navigate the complexities of entrepreneurship, set realistic goals, and develop the necessary skills and mindset for success. Mentoring can be done formally or informally, through one-on-one mentoring relationships, group mentoring programs, or by participating in entrepreneurship programs or events.

2. **Sharing Your Story:** Sharing your own entrepreneurial story, including your successes, failures, and lessons learned, can be inspiring and motivating for aspiring entrepreneurs. It can help them understand the challenges and realities of entrepreneurship, and provide valuable insights and inspiration for their own journey. You can share your story through speaking engagements, writing articles or blogs, participating in interviews or podcasts, or leveraging social media platforms.

3. **Providing Access to Resources:** Providing access to resources, such as funding, networks, or expertise, can be a significant way to support aspiring entrepreneurs. This can include offering mentorship or advice on fundraising, connecting them with potential investors or partners, or providing access to your own networks or contacts. By leveraging your resources, you can help aspiring entrepreneurs overcome barriers and accelerate their entrepreneurial journey.

4. **Creating Entrepreneurial Programs or Initiatives:** Creating entrepreneurial programs or initiatives can be a proactive way to inspire and support the next generation of entrepreneurs. This can include establishing scholarships or grants for aspiring entrepreneurs, organizing entrepreneurship competitions or events, or partnering with educational institutions to develop entrepreneurship curriculum or workshops. By creating opportunities for aspiring entrepreneurs to learn, connect, and grow, you can contribute to the development of a vibrant entrepreneurial ecosystem.

## Conclusion

In conclusion, social responsibility is a crucial aspect of entrepreneurship that goes beyond just financial success. It involves making a positive impact on the community and society, giving back, and paying it forward to inspire the next generation of entrepreneurs. By integrating social responsibility into their business practices, entrepreneurs can contribute to a more sustainable, inclusive, and successful entrepreneurial ecosystem.

## Chapter 14 Takeaways

Giving back and paying it forward are essential aspects of social responsibility in entrepreneurship. By making a positive impact on your community and society, you can contribute to a more sustainable and inclusive future. Here are some key takeaways:

1.  Social responsibility should be an integral part of entrepreneurship. It goes beyond just making profits and encompasses the impact a business has on the community and society at large.

2.  Giving back can take many forms, including charitable donations, volunteer work, social entrepreneurship, and environmental sustainability efforts. Entrepreneurs should consider various ways to make a positive impact that align with their values and business goals.

3.  Social responsibility can benefit entrepreneurs and their businesses in multiple ways, including enhancing reputation, attracting customers and investors, fostering employee engagement, and creating long-term sustainability.

4. Collaborations and partnerships can amplify the impact of social responsibility efforts by pooling resources, expertise, and networks. Working with other businesses, organizations, and stakeholders can lead to more effective and scalable solutions to societal challenges.

5. Mentoring and coaching aspiring entrepreneurs, sharing your story, and providing access to resources can be powerful ways to pay it forward and inspire the next generation of entrepreneurs. Supporting aspiring entrepreneurs can contribute to the growth and success of the entrepreneurial ecosystem.

6. Social responsibility should be integrated into the business strategy and operations, rather than just being an afterthought. Entrepreneurs should be intentional in their efforts to give back and make a positive impact, considering the needs of the community and society, and aligning their actions with their business values and goals.

7. Social responsibility is an ongoing commitment. Entrepreneurs should continuously assess and measure the impact of their efforts, and be open to feedback and improvement. It is important to approach social responsibility as a journey, and strive for continuous improvement and innovation.

# Chapter 15

# Conclusion

## Encouragement for Readers to Unlock Their Full Potential for Success in Entrepreneurship

Congratulations! You have reached the conclusion of "The Unstoppable Entrepreneur: Unlocking Your Full Potential for Success." Let's take a moment in this final chapter to reflect on your journey to becoming an unstoppable entrepreneur, summarize the key lessons and takeaways, and encourage you to keep unlocking your full potential for success in entrepreneurship.

## Reflections on the Road to Unstoppable Entrepreneurship

Entrepreneurship is a remarkable journey that necessitates courage, determination, and resilience. Take a moment to acknowledge the progress you've made, the challenges you've overcome, and the lessons you've learned as you reflect on your own journey. Remember the thrill of starting your own business, the rush of pursuing your passion, and the satisfaction of your accomplishments. Reflecting on your journey can give you a sense of accomplishment and motivation to continue on your entrepreneurial journey.

## Summarizing Key Takeaways and Lessons

Throughout "The Unstoppable Entrepreneur," we've looked

at various lessons and takeaways that can help you succeed. Let us summarize some of the most important findings:

1. **Adopt an Entrepreneurial Mindset:** Entrepreneurship success begins with the right mindset. Adopt a growth mindset, be open to learning, be resilient, and be optimistic in the face of challenges and failures. Have faith in yourself and your ability to overcome challenges.

2. **Clarify Your Purpose and Vision:** Define your purpose and vision and allow them to guide your decisions and actions. Your purpose and vision serve as a compass, guiding you and motivating you to achieve your objectives.

3. **Set SMART Goals:** To guide your actions and track your progress, set specific, measurable, achievable, relevant, and time-bound (SMART) goals. To stay focused and motivated, review and adjust your goals on a regular basis.

4. **Create a Solid Foundation:** Create a solid foundation for your business by conducting extensive market research, understanding your target audience, developing a unique value proposition, and creating a comprehensive business plan. A solid foundation lays the groundwork for long-term growth.

5. **Develop Effective Leadership Skills:** Effective leadership skills are essential for entrepreneurs. Develop

your leadership abilities by inspiring and motivating your team, creating a positive work environment, and making strategic decisions. A strong leader can motivate their team to achieve success.

6. **Embrace Innovation and Adaptability:** Make innovation and adaptability core business principles. Be willing to pivot and adapt your strategies in response to new ideas, technologies, and market changes. Staying relevant and competitive requires innovation and adaptability.

7. **Develop Strategic Partnerships:** Work with other businesses, organizations, and stakeholders to expand your network, gain access to resources, and effectively scale your business. Strategic alliances can open doors to new markets and opportunities for growth.

8. **Invest in Marketing and Branding:** Create a solid marketing and branding strategy to promote your company, raise brand awareness, and attract customers. To stand out in a crowded market, use a variety of marketing channels and consistently communicate your unique value proposition.

9. **Manage Your Finances Wisely:** Proper financial management is critical for your company's long-term success. Create a budget, manage cash flow, and make informed financial decisions to ensure your company's

financial health. Financial management that is sound can provide stability and sustainability.

10. **Develop Strong Customer Relationships:** Develop strong customer relationships by providing exceptional products, services, and customer experiences. Prioritize customer satisfaction and use feedback to improve your offerings over time. Customers who are pleased with your products or services are more likely to become advocates for your company.

11. **Maintain a Healthy Work-Life Balance:** Entrepreneurship can be demanding, so it's critical to keep a healthy work-life balance. Take physical, mental, and emotional care of yourself, and make time for personal interests, hobbies, and relationships. Work-life balance can improve your overall well-being and success as an entrepreneur.

12. **Learn from Failures:** Failure is an inevitable part of the entrepreneurial journey, and failures should be viewed as learning opportunities. Accept failure as a stepping stone to success, analyze what went wrong, and use the lessons learned to improve and grow. Take calculated risks and learn from both your successes and failures.

13. **Surround Yourself with a Supportive Network:** Surround yourself with a supportive network of mentors, advisors, peers, and friends who can offer advice,

feedback, and encouragement. Having a strong support system can help you navigate obstacles, stay motivated, and grow as an entrepreneur.

14. **Maintain Persistence and Resilience:** Starting a business is not always easy, and there will be setbacks along the way. Maintain your perseverance and resilience in the face of adversity. Continue to push forward, stay focused on your objectives, and never give up on your dreams.

## Encouragement to Readers to Unlock Their Full Entrepreneurial Potential

As you reflect on your entrepreneurial journey and internalize the key lessons and takeaways, keep in mind that reaching your full potential for success is an ongoing process. Entrepreneurship is a dynamic and ever-changing field that necessitates ongoing learning, adaptation, and perseverance. Here's some motivation to keep you going on your entrepreneurial journey:

1. **Believe in Yourself:** As an entrepreneur, you have the skills, talents, and determination to succeed. Have faith in yourself and your abilities. Believe in your instincts, take calculated risks, and have faith in your vision and goals.

2. **View Obstacles as Opportunities:** Obstacles are unavoidable in business, but they also present

opportunities for growth and learning. Accept challenges as chances to grow, innovate, and become a better entrepreneur. Don't avoid challenges; instead, face them with resilience and determination.

3. **Continue Learning and Innovating:** Entrepreneurship is a constantly changing field, and it is critical to continue learning and innovating in order to stay ahead. Maintain your curiosity, seek out new information, and keep your skills and strategies up to date. In your entrepreneurial journey, embrace a culture of continuous learning and improvement.

4. **Establish a Strong Support Network:** Surround yourself with a supportive network of mentors, advisors, peers, and friends who can offer advice, feedback, and encouragement. Develop relationships with like-minded people who can inspire, challenge, and support you on your entrepreneurial journey.

5. **Maintain Focus on Your Purpose and Vision:** Your purpose and vision will drive your entrepreneurial journey. Maintain your focus on your purpose and vision and allow them to guide your decisions and actions. Be adaptable while maintaining your core values and long-term goals.

6. **Maintain Resilience and Persistence:** Entrepreneurship is difficult, and there will be ups and downs along the way. Maintain your resilience and

persistence in the face of obstacles, setbacks, and failures. Learn from your mistakes, stay focused on your objectives, and keep moving forward.

7. **Recognize Your Successes:** Don't forget to recognize your accomplishments, no matter how minor they may appear. Recognize your accomplishments, acknowledge your progress, and give yourself credit for your hard work and dedication. Celebrating your accomplishments can help you stay motivated and inspired.

8. **Maintain Your Passion and Authenticity:** Passion and authenticity are powerful drivers of entrepreneurship success. Maintain your integrity, values, and passions. Maintain your entrepreneurial spirit and allow your authenticity to shine through in your business endeavors.

To summarize, becoming an unstoppable entrepreneur is a journey that necessitates self-awareness, ongoing learning, perseverance, and a growth mindset. It's not always easy, but it's always worthwhile. You can maximize your chances of success in entrepreneurship by reflecting on your journey and internalizing the key lessons and takeaways.

Remember to prioritize your mindset and beliefs, cultivate a positive and resilient attitude, and view failures as opportunities to learn. Continuously improve your skills, stay focused on your purpose and vision, and surround yourself with a strong support system. Maintain your authenticity, passion, and perseverance in pursuing your entrepreneurial dreams.

Remember to maintain a healthy work-life balance, take care of your well-being, and celebrate your successes as you navigate the challenges and opportunities of entrepreneurship. Surround yourself with people who will inspire and support you, and never stop learning and innovating.

As an entrepreneur, you have the potential to achieve great things. Accept the journey, stay committed to your goals, and continue to realize your full potential for success. You can become an unstoppable entrepreneur and create a meaningful and fulfilling entrepreneurial journey if you have the right mindset, skills, and support.

# ABOUT THE BOOK

"The Unstoppable Entrepreneur: Unlocking Your Full Potential for Success" is a guide designed to empower aspiring and current entrepreneurs with the mindset, strategies, and skills to overcome challenges, maximize opportunities, and achieve their goals. The book covers a wide range of topics in 15 chapters, including discovering one's passion, building a growth mindset, setting clear goals, conducting market research, analyzing the competition, creating a solid business model, building a personal brand, mastering time management, developing resilience, grit, and managing stress. The book also emphasizes the significance of social responsibility, giving back, and inspiring the next generation of entrepreneurs. Overall, the book provides practical insights, strategies, and tools for success in the dynamic world of entrepreneurship, encouraging readers to reflect on their entrepreneurial journey and become unstoppable entrepreneurs.